THAT'S A WRAP

THAT'S A WRAP

How Movies Are Made

FOREWORD BY DAVID MAMET

BY NED DOWD ◆ PHOTOGRAPHS BY HENRY HORENSTEIN

SILVER BURDETT PRESS

This book is for Ollie Hallowell—HH
and Robert Altman—ND

This book is a combined effort of so many generous parties. Special thanks goes to the book doctor, Marjorie Prager, for her attentions and David Mamet for his introduction. Thanks also to Nelson Films, Inc., David Giler, Graham Henderson, Jeffrey Balsmeyer, Ollie Hallowell, Ellie Hollinshead, Joe Langis for Spectrum Color Labs, Marie Weismiller Wallace, Pam Pollack, Sylvia Frezzolini, and, of course, Tracy Hill.

Photograph on page 50 © Marie Weismiller Wallace

SILVER BURDETT PRESS
A Division of
Paramount Publishing
250 James Street
Morristown, New Jersey 07960

10 9 8 7 6 5 4 3 2 1

Library of Congress Cataloging–in–Publication Data: Dowd, Ned. That's a wrap: how movies are made/by Ned Dowd: photographs by Henry Horenstein. Summary: Describes the many steps involved in developing and filming a motion picture and preparing it for release. Motion pictures — Production and direction — Juvenile literature. [1. Motion pictures — Production and direction.] I. Horenstein, Henry. ill. II. Title. PN1995.9.P7D69 1991 791.43'0232 — dc 20 91-6435 AC ISBN: 0-382-24376-5

Foreword

I remember we were filming on a Chicago residential street. An elderly lady walked out of her house, down the street, through the lights and cables, and past the grips and electricians and the rest of us.

She was shaking her head as she walked, and muttering, "With as little work as the bunch of you are doing, you ought to be in Washington. What a bunch of loafers."

More than offended, I was astounded by her comments. What was she talking about? I looked around and saw 60 people working their tails off. What did she see? She didn't know what to look for, and, so, had walked right through the most interesting and unusual work environment, and had seen nothing.

Maybe it's like watching the life in a tidepool—you have to get close, and you have to know what you're looking for.

Movie workers are the hardest working and the most spirited people it has ever been my pleasure to work with. The spirit on a set is: "Do it right, do it now, help the other guy, enjoy yourself."

I love the life on the set. I often think that it is the modern equivalent of a cattle drive: a bunch of folks get together for three months, work hard, play hard, sleep little, and take a lot of pride in seeing the thing through. A working set is a terrific place to be. I had the great good fortune to have been personally initiated into its mysteries by Ned Dowd, who now, in this book, gives you a most excellent tour backstage.

DAVID MAMET
Cambridge, MA
February, 1991

W elcome to a place that doesn't really exist.

The street is fake. The buildings are fake. The trees are made out of plaster. And what appears to be late afternoon on Rodeo Drive in Beverly Hills, California, is actually early morning in the middle of the Mexican desert.

These people are part of the cast and crew of *The Taking of Beverly Hills,* and together—working twelve hours a day, six or even seven days a week—they will create a feature film.

You might recognize the star of the movie (the guy in the No. 12 football jersey and baseball cap) or the man in the police uniform; but there are close to two hundred people you won't recognize on a movie set: the women and men whose work takes place *behind* the scenes.

Let's take an insider's look at how a movie is made to see how the "unreal" winds up looking absolutely "real" when we're sitting in the dark, gazing wide-eyed at the cinema screen.

Phase One

DEVELOPMENT

A movie begins with an idea. Sometimes a writer will create a script or screenplay, based on his or her own idea and will try to find a movie producer who is willing to raise the money, from individuals called backers or "angels" or from investment companies, to turn the script into a film. But very often, a producer buys the rights to film a bestselling book or uses an event that really happened, and hires a writer to turn existing ideas into screenplay form.

Writers, working alone or in teams, often start by putting down their idea in an outline or a written treatment, a brief synopsis of the story that is only a few pages long. Using this very short version, writers talk up their film idea at meetings, trying to get a producer or a movie studio excited enough about the script to put up the money to back the film.

Many people hire an agent to make movie deals for them. Agents usually suggest specific actors who they think would be good to play the major parts in the movie, and propose a director for the film. When one agent represents all these people—writers, actors, and director—he or she is said to be packaging a movie deal.

The development phase ends when a deal with a producer is made and a budget is approved. Budgets for feature films range from $5 million to $50 million...and the producer is responsible for watching every penny!

The producer and the production manager will oversee the practical side of planning for the movie: Where will the film be shot? How will the equipment and people get there? They will run things on a daily basis, deciding how to spend the money in the budget.

Escaping gas HISSES into the night. It gives him an idea.

KELVIN
Well, then I just dreamed us out of
here. Hold the fort.

Kelvin dashes now, ahead of the BULLDOZERS. Grabs a GARDEN
HOSE and couples it onto the gas jet from a lamp.

OTHER GAS LAMPS all FLICKER suddenly, and then go OUT.
Kelvin grabs the other end of the hose and dives into

A SPRINKLER TRENCH

Kelvin yanks the plastic pipe free, JAMS the hose ONTO IT.
He runs, dodging fire from the charging bulldozers,

Kelvin goes back to the gas jet, turns a valve near the
ground, and a PRESSURE NEEDLE RISES.

OUTSIDE - HECTOR - WITH THE BULLDOZERS

He hears a sudden HISSING from the sprinkler heads --
Hector wrinkles his nose, SMELLING GAS--

Now, he sees Kelvin - grabbing a flare gun from the machine
gun nest -- and Hector SUDDENLY UNDERSTANDS...

HECTOR
Back off!! Get down!!!

KELVIN - FIRING THE FLARE GUN

WHHHOOOOMMM! SPRINKLER HEADS EXPLODING INTO FLAMING TORCHES

EPA MEN are burning, twisting, screaming --

VARNEY POV - THE INFERNO

The entire battleground ERUPTING like a DOZEN VOLCANOS. One
of the bulldozers is completely fried.

Varney screams at his troops, but they scatter in panic.

THE LEAD BULLDOZER
rolls on, making it past the edge of the fire.
But the BULLDOZER DRIVER is HIT. He falls off, and the
machine stops.

...ING SANTA MONICA - ENTERING RODEO DRIVE

...ing it, slams through the intersection
...hower of sparks.

...ELVIN
...get past Varney's
...h this thing.

...he sound of ROTORS approaching.

...HOPPER SWOOPING DOWN

...m, sealing off the block.

...COPTER

...ing U-TURN. The
...Santa Monica Blvd.

...sing the distance

...blowing out

...y when

...ne

...ad.

...police and fire

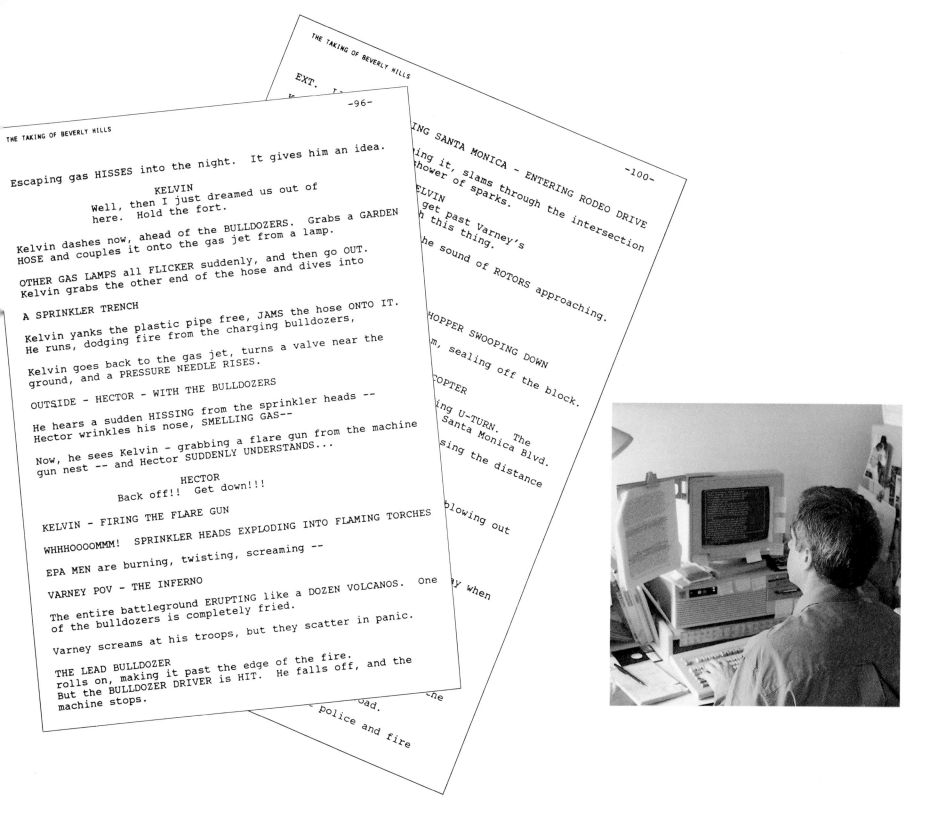

Phase Two

PRE-PRODUCTION

During the second phase of moviemaking, the film's producer and director work with the writer to revise and refine the script.

A movie script contains dialogue, which are the words the actors speak in the film; information about the characters, such as age, size, hair color, clothes, habits, likes and dislikes; and technical directions about scenery, camera angles, and lighting. Sometimes, a script will be changed each time a new movie star considers acting in the film to make it fit his or her personality or style better.

During pre-production, important crew members are hired, too. They will begin thinking about how the film should look and sound.

The producer hires a casting director, who is in charge of finding the right person to play each part called for in the script. Actors audition many times. They read lines together and are screen-tested to see how they will look on the big screen. Actors often say that the worst thing about their job is being rejected again and again, being told, "You're just not right for this part" because they are too young, old, short, tall, fat, skinny—"too" something!

The director also chooses a director of photography whose style of camera work suits the screenplay. Some are known for creating dark and menacing moods, others for making scenes look as if they had been painted. The D. P., sometimes called a cinematographer, decides how to compose and light each shot in the film, and oversees the work of the camera operator and the lighting crew.

A production designer makes sure that the "look" of the film is what the director had in mind. For example, in this movie the director wanted to recreate a street in Beverly Hills in Mexico. The designer hires an art director, who will be in charge of building the sets on which the film will be shot. The designer will also hire a construction foreman and together they will hire other crew members who will work together as a unit.

Following the production designer's direction, the art department creates drawings of the sets. These are turned into blueprints for the carpenters and painters on the crew to use during construction. Sets of rooms are usually built with fewer than four walls and without a ceiling. This way, the camera can be positioned wherever the director wants it in order to get a different view of the scene. When only the front wall of a set is built, it is called a facade. Some walls are designed to be removable; they are called wild walls.

The director works with the art department to create a storyboard. This is a sketched version of how the movie will unfold, scene by scene. By using the storyboard, the director can plan camera angles and decide how the individual shots will be pieced together. The crew members can refer to the storyboard as they build the sets and plan stunts and special effects.

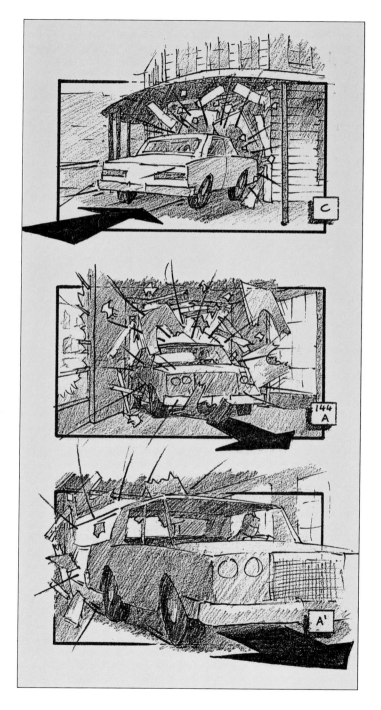

The costumes are just as important as the sets. The right costume can help an actor become the character he or she plays. As the sets are being built, the costume designer sketches the clothes that will be worn in each scene of the film by the major actors. After the actors are chosen, measurements are taken and fittings are done to make sure everything will look as good on the actor as it did on paper. The wardrobe department often makes more than one copy of important costumes so that the filming will not be held up if a dress or jacket gets dirty or damaged. An elaborate costume can cost as much as $25,000!

Phase Three
PRODUCTION

Production, the third phase of moviemaking, is also called principal photography. This is the time when most filming actually happens. When a movie is shot in a real place rather than on a sound stage or sound-proof set in a studio, it is said to be shot on location.

Location scouting is done to find the best place to shoot the movie.

Very often, one location will "stand in" for another, because it is cheaper to shoot there or just because it is more convenient. In this film, the set in Mexico is standing in for the real Rodeo Drive.

For example, it was important to choose a remote and empty spot when shooting *The Taking of Beverly Hills* because the script called for explosions and gunfire. In fact, an entire section of a real street, Rodeo Drive, was recreated in the Mexican desert just so it could be blown up!

Once the location is selected, everything is brought there by truck. Actors use motor homes and trailers as their dressing rooms. The crew uses one of the trucks as a place where they can rest, change, or use the bathroom.

Many sets are built entirely on location. Others are brought from the studio set shop and have finishing touches added up until the moment the camera is turned on. Fiberglass trees, leaves, and plants are added to make false fronts and phony buildings look more real. However, once the shooting is over, things go right back to the way they were before the film crew arrived.

S ets are filled only with the things the camera will see. Areas that are out of camera range are left empty. The furniture and objects that make a place look lived in are chosen by the set decorator.

Every scene must be lit correctly in order to make sure that the lighting is consistent from shot to shot, and to create the mood and look agreed upon by the director and cinematographer. The person in charge of lighting a scene is called the gaffer. This word comes from an old European carnival term for herding, or gaffing, the crowd into a tent. The assistant, who orders all the equipment and keeps the lighting crew hard at work, is called the best boy. This is

an odd name that probably originated during the early days of filmmaking, when the gaffer chose the kid on the crew who was "best" at keeping everybody else hopping.

Many different kinds of lights are used in making a movie; and filters and gels let the electricians who operate the lamps change the color and intensity of the lighting, shot by shot. Scrims or silks are positioned wherever they are needed on the set. These materials either diffuse or reflect the light.

Grips (called this because they "get a grip" on pieces of equipment) are the people who move things around on the set. They put up material to diffuse or bounce the light from the lamps, and reposition walls and props from scene to scene. The head grip is called the key grip.

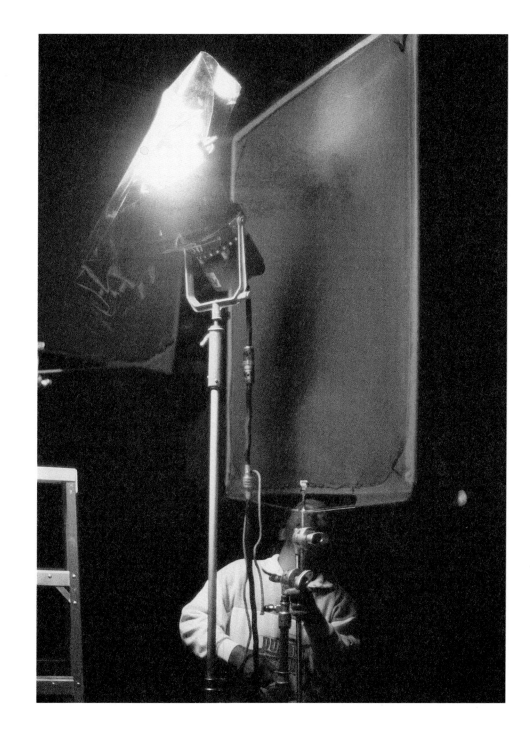

Sound is recorded onto audio tape, not directly onto the film being shot. It is kept separate for several reasons. In this way, for example, the actors' dialogue can be changed and replaced. Later, the words will be mixed with music and sound effects to match the action shown on screen to make the best possible sound track.

The sound designer oversees the entire movie sound track. He or she selects a sound mixer, who is in charge of recording sound while on location. The man shown here has a powerful tape recorder and a mixing board set up on a sound cart just a few yards away from the set. He listens through headphones to the signals picked up by microphones planted on the set and by long-handled boom microphones held above the actors' heads by a boom operator.

Scenes are often filmed from several different angles, with actors close to the camera or at a distance. When these shots are combined eventually, the sound from each shot must match what we see on film in order to give the impression that the actors are speaking from close up or from far away, even if they were not. The sound mixer adjusts the levels of the actors' voices, mixing in background sound, or ambience, to create the impression of a real place. You might hear crickets chirping, birds singing or the traffic zooming by a busy intersection.

Before the actors appear on the set, they change into their costumes in the trailer that serves as a dressing room. Everything has to be just right. The wardrobe department checks to make sure that accessories such as jewelry, glasses, handbags, and shoes are all from the right era, and makes last-minute adjustments to the way costumes fit.

Just before shooting starts, the actors go to the makeup trailer. Makeup artists and hair stylists make minor adjustments on the set between shots. Makeup can be subtle or dramatic, and can help a character grow old before our eyes or go from hairy to bald! Sometimes, when scenes are shot on the same day but must seem to be several weeks apart in the movie, the actors have to get made up in different ways over and over again.

The makeup artist can also turn a healthy actor into the walking wounded—dripping blood, oozing gore, bullet wounds—if that's what is called for in the script.

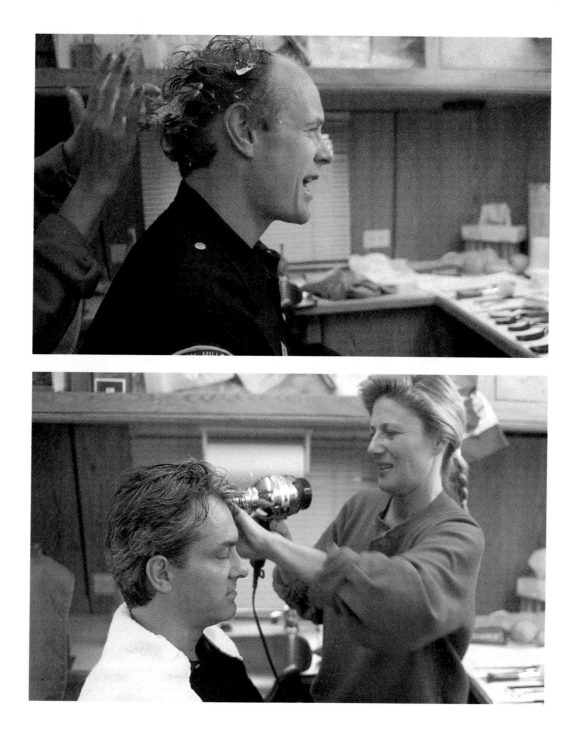

While the actors are in makeup, there's a call for extras. Extras are the people you see in the background of a scene, walking by, eating in a restaurant, driving down the block, filling a stadium for a ball game or a rock concert. They do what is called background action. Extras can make a movie seem much more real. The casting director hires extras who look right for the film—clean-cut, exotic, sophisticated, frightening, or even weird. Sometimes extras have to wear costumes from another era; more often, they appear in their own clothes.

Before the camera begins rolling, the actors rehearse. Even when a movie is full of stunts and special effects, actors must make it all seem real. It's the director's job to help each actor give the best possible performance, interpreting the words and actions in the script to convey how each character feels in that scene. He or she works hard to keep the actors focused and involved. This is not an easy task since so many technical processes are going on at the same time that the actors are trying to give a great performance.

When everything is ready—the camera is in position, the lighting is perfect, the actors are on their marks (places marked with tape or chalk to show exactly where to stand in each shot)—the assistant director yells, "Quiet on the set!"

The assistant director, or A.D., is the manager of the set. He or she schedules when the cast and crew report for work, what each day's shooting will include, what time the actors have to report to makeup, and when the company breaks for meals. All this information is put together on a call sheet that is given out at the end of the day for the next day's work.

The A.D. keeps in touch with the crew by walkie-talkie; tells the extras what to do and when to do it; and, after checking with the director, goes through a routine that begins every take—each time the camera is turned on—in a movie. First, the A.D. yells, "Camera!" and the camera operator responds by saying, "Ready!" Then the A.D. calls, "Roll sound!" and the sound mixer yells, "Speed!" when the tape recorder is going.

Everybody knows that the time has come for absolute silence—a take is about to begin.

When the camera is turned on, the first thing photographed is a slate. This is a small, hinged blackboard that contains the name of the film, the date, the director's name or initials, and the scene, shot, and take number. This information will be crucial later, during the editing process. The person holding the slate in front of the camera slaps the slate closed, saying, "Marker!" This puts a loud, clapping noise on the sound track when the two halves of the slate come together on the film. By lining up what is seen with what is heard, the film editor knows that the picture and sound are in sync—lined up exactly in synchronization—and moving together at the same time. If two cameras are rolling during a scene, there are two slates. There are three slates for three cameras, and so on.

Sometimes the camera remains in one position on a three-legged stand called sticks, or a tripod, while the actors in a scene move around. The focus puller constantly refocuses the camera lens as actors move closer to or farther away from the camera. For shots in which the actors stand still and the camera moves, the camera is mounted on a wheeled platform called a dolly and pulled by a dolly grip along tracks that have been laid in advance. When an aerial view is needed, the camera is mounted on a crane that is similar to the cherry picker used in telephone line repair.

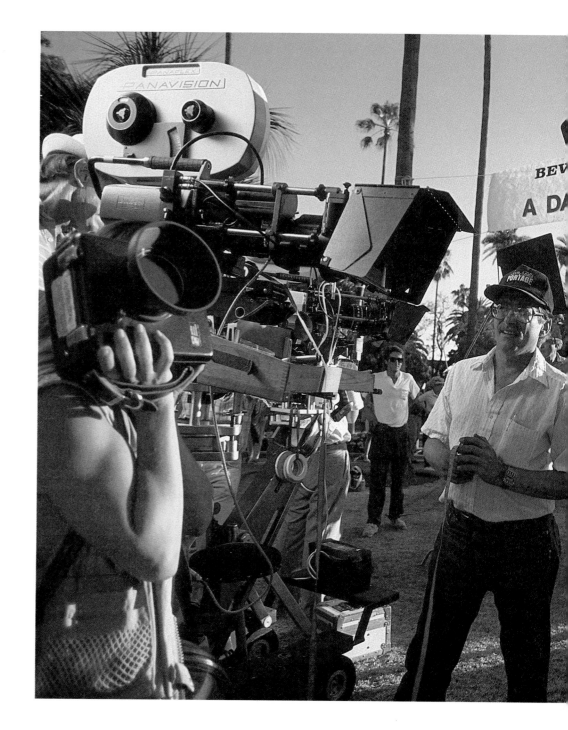

With the camera and tape recorder rolling, the actors begin to play the scene. Technicians check the sound recording levels and make adjustments as the scene progresses. When the shot is completed, the director yells, "Cut!"

If the director is satisfied with the performance of the actors, he or she says "print it." If another take is necessary—because someone flubbed a line of dialogue, the camera operator noticed a piece of dirt on the lens, the roar of a plane or the siren of an ambulance spoiled sound recording, or a prop didn't work correctly—the actors and crew go back to their original positions and start again. Sometimes as many as a hundred takes are needed to get a shot exactly right. If you're lucky, the first take is perfect.

At the end of the day's shooting, the film is rushed to the lab and printed. The director and the film editor watch these rushes, or dailies, every night so they can see how things are going and make suggestions that might improve the actors' performances and the work of the technical crew.

Some shots are simple, involving only one or two people and very little action; but others call for many extras and complicated movement. In this scene, thirty or so kid extras get to tackle the star of the film, who plays a football hero named "Boomer" Hayes. The kids have to look perfect, right down to the way their shoelaces are tied.

No matter in what order they appear in the film, all the scenes that take place on one set are shot one after another. Sometimes, a scene that is supposed to take place at night is shot during daylight hours. This is called shooting day for night. This saves time and money, but it makes it harder for the actors to keep track of what their characters are supposed to be thinking and feeling at different points in the movie.

As each take is filmed and recorded, a script supervisor follows along in the screenplay, making very detailed notes about how things look and sound. If an actor crosses his or her legs at the end of a take, or if a glass of water goes from full to empty during the course of a shot, it's the script supervisor's job to notice and mark it down for the film editor to see. This is called continuity. Watch carefully the next time you're at the movies; you just might catch a continuity mistake.

Most movie crews include a second unit. This is almost a crew-within-a-crew that shoots action that is secondary to the main scenes: car chases, crowds at a ball game, people eating in a restaurant. This unit has its own director, technicians, schedule, and script supervisor.

ot everything on a movie set is exciting and glamorous. In fact, life on location can be downright boring. Actors wait many hours to be called to do just a few seconds' work. Then the crew must set up for another shot, which takes time and means more waiting. People pass the time during their long delays by playing cards, embroidering, swapping stories, and thinking about what's for lunch… which might be served at midnight, if night shooting is taking place.

A professional catering company working out of a truck serves meal after meal. The truck houses a full kitchen, complete with a griddle for frying eggs for breakfast. And when the crew is hungry, watch out!

There's always food available at the craft service table. When someone stops by for a cold drink or a quick snack, it is called grazing, because, like a cow or sheep, he or she eats standing up.

Have you ever wondered how scenes that take place in moving cars are shot? An insert car, a truck fitted with a camera platform in the rear, tows the picture car, the vehicle being filmed, while an actor in the driver's seat pretends to drive or hold a conversation. It's a tight fit, but the director, the A.D., the camera operator, a makeup artist, a hair stylist, the sound mixer, the script supervisor, and the key grip usually manage to squeeze on the insert car.

Sometimes a scene calls for rain and the streets must stay looking wet for many hours. High-tech water trucks can wet down miles of roads in a matter of seconds.

tunts and special effects make movies exciting and suspenseful. The stunt coordinator's job is to make what looks like total mayhem on film—explosions, hurricanes, earthquakes, four-alarm fires, bloody murders, and spectacular car crashes—safe and under control during the filming.

Specially trained stuntmen and stuntwomen take the actors' places during highly athletic or risky sequences. When a stunt is too dangerous even for someone with training and experience, dummies are used.

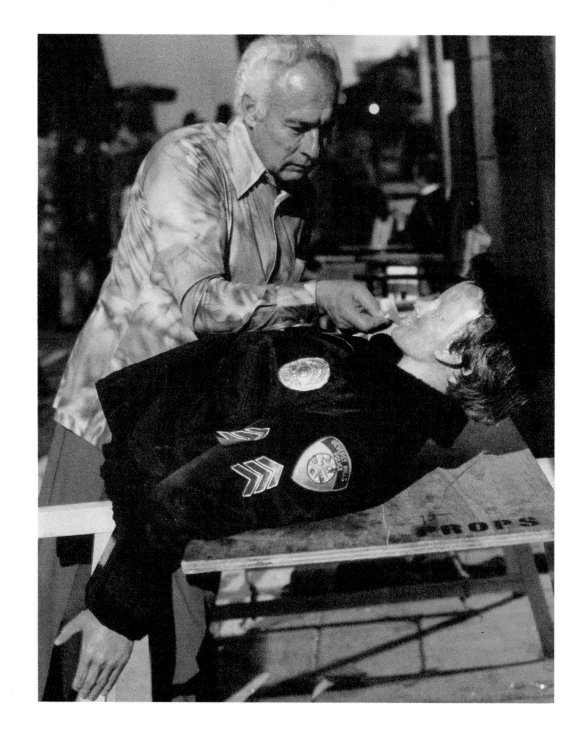

If a stunt involves gunfire, sometimes it is necessary to show a person being shot. To create the appearance of a bullet wound, an actor is fitted with a squib. This is a tiny pouch containing an explosive material. While the actor pretends to be shot, an off-camera technician pushes a button to explode the squib. The squib should go off just as the blank fired by the on-screen gun hits the actor, who may also be rigged with small pouches of fake blood that release at the same time.

The story of *The Taking of Beverly Hills* revolves around the staging of a fake toxic waste disaster. In the story, an explosion is set off by crooks to give them the perfect cover for a gigantic robbery. While the citizens of Beverly Hills flee in panic, the burglars clean out every store on swanky Rodeo Drive.

To make the explosion and the fires it spawns seem real on film, the special effects team carefully plans and rehearses every shot, making sure there is no danger to anyone. The cast and crew wear protective clothing and keep a safe distance away from the fires and explosions during the filming.

The Taking of Beverly Hills used 1,500 pounds of explosives and 20,000 rounds of blank ammunition to pull off its dramatic special effects!

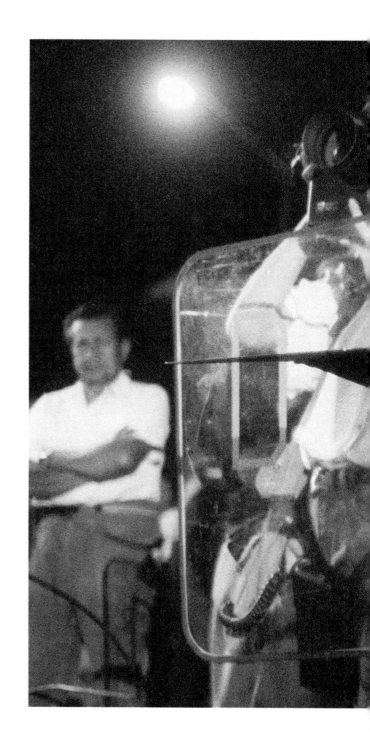

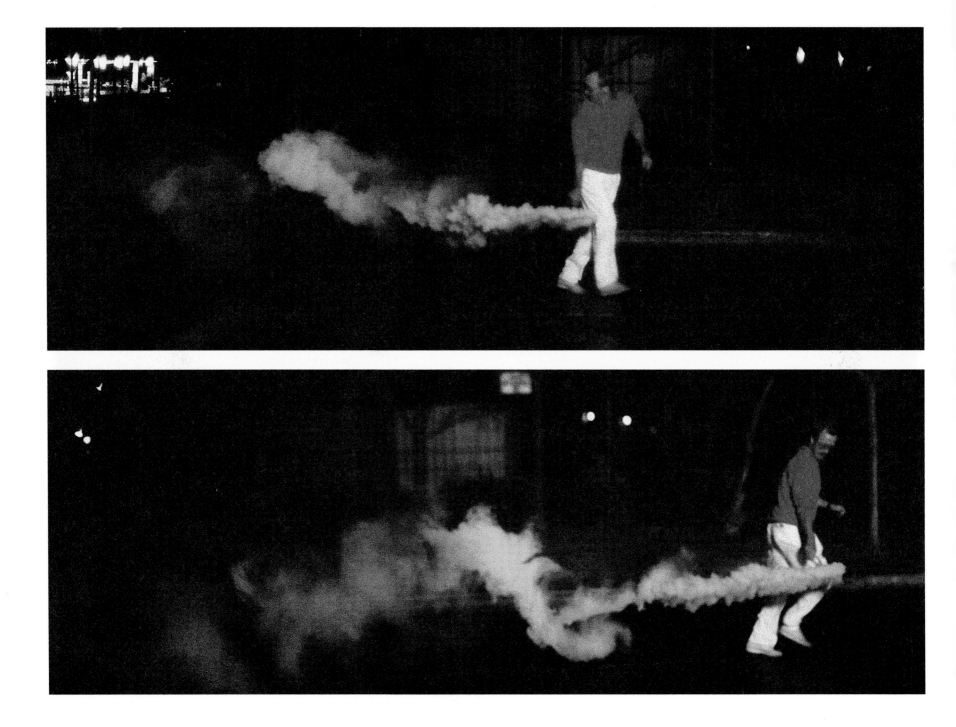

When everything comes together, magic happens on screen. We may know that what we see in most films isn't real, but we are so wrapped up in the story, the action, and the special effects, that we suspend our disbelief and just get lost in the movie.

That's a wrap! Once the shooting has been completed, the set can be struck, or dismantled, and trucked away, and the Mexican desert can go back to playing itself, not standing in for California. The cast and crew have a big party to celebrate the end of principal photography before going their separate ways, usually on to the next movie to be made.

POST-PRODUCTION

After shooting has been completed, the final phase of film-making begins. This is called post-production, and it usually takes many months, compared to the fifteen-week shooting schedule typical of most movies.

Once all the film is in the can, the film editor must make the individual shots into a story and select the best takes of each shot. Since scenes have been shot out of sequence, the editor depends on the notes taken by the script supervisor as well as on reference marks—tiny code numbers imprinted onto the film and audio tape —to help keep track of what might be 120 miles of film. That means the editor whittles down eighty hours of screen time to about ninety minutes. The rest winds up on the cutting room floor as the editor splices and tapes together the pieces that make up the final "cut" of the film.

At the daily screening of the rushes on location, the editor and the director had discussed which takes they liked best. Now, in the editing room, the editor and the assistants put the film together from those takes. The editor chooses angles that he or she feels work more effectively to show off an actor's performance or feature the action in the scene. He or she also adds cutaways, which are shots that show details such as a close-up of someone's hands, and reaction shots, which show the response of other characters in the scene.

At the same time the film editor is at work, sound editors create and record sound effects and a composer writes and records the score for the film, sometimes using a complete orchestra. Music adds emotion and excitement to any movie. Films often use well-known popular music, especially rock 'n' roll, to create a mood instantly. Many movies that take place in the not-so-distant past use oldies to make audiences remember the way they felt when they were teenagers during the 1950s and 1960s.

The first completed edit of a movie, with the sound effects and music added in exactly the right places, is called the rough cut. The director and producer screen it and decide what needs to be changed, emphasized, or even rewritten and reshot. The version of the film that is released to movie theaters, the final cut, can still be weeks or months away.

Once everyone approves the final cut, prints are made of the film. The first, or test, print is called an answer print. The director and the film editor check to make sure the movie looks just the way they wanted it to look. Any necessary corrections are made, and then release prints are made and distributed.

How long does it take to complete a movie? That differs from film to film, of course. However, as the editing comes to an end, the studio that is distributing the film begins to run an advertising campaign on television and in newspapers and magazines. "Coming attractions" showing clips from the movie are put together to give moviegoers a glimpse of the film. Advertising budgets can sometimes be bigger than the budgets of the movies themselves!

The film studio rents many copies of the finished film to movie theaters across the country, even around the world. Publicity, public appearances by the actors, movie reviews in the media, and word-of-mouth recommendations from people who've seen the film can make the movie a success, or break it.

Will the film win an Oscar or disappear overnight into oblivion? Only time will tell. But the people who made this movie are undoubtedly already hard at work on the next one, living out of trailers, memorizing their lines, or thinking up more terrifying stunts, somewhere... behind the scenes.